THE STORY
OF THE
OLYMPICS

Minna Lacey

Illustrated by
Paddy Mounter

Reading Consultant: Alison Kelly
Roehampton University

Contents

Chapter 1

Sports in ancient Greece

The ancient Greeks loved to compete. They held contests for everything — public speaking, painting, writing, even kissing.

But the most popular competitions were for sports, such as running, chariot racing, boxing, wrestling or throwing the discus*.

* A round stone

Any big event was a good excuse for a sports contest. The Greeks held races and wrestling matches at feasts and religious festivals – and funerals too.

They even took javelins and discuses with them when they went to war.

Chapter 2

The first Games

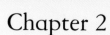

No one is sure how
the Olympic Games really
began, but the first recorded
sports event at Olympia took place
in 776BC*, about 3,000 years ago.

* BC stands for 'Before Christ'. Dates marked 'BC' are
counted backwards from the birth of Christ.

Olympia was in a beautiful river valley, surrounded by olive groves and low hills in southwest Greece.

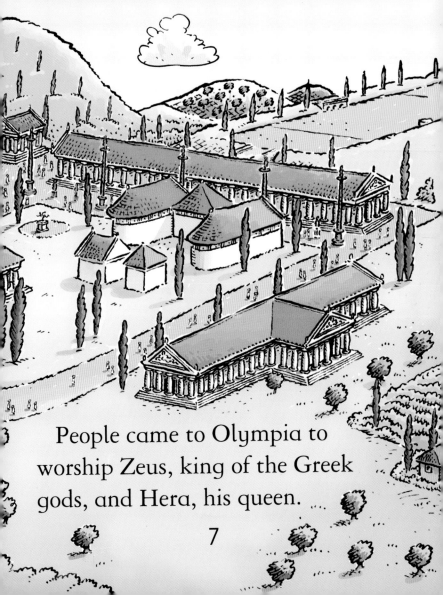

People came to Olympia to worship Zeus, king of the Greek gods, and Hera, his queen.

One story says that it was Zeus's son, the Greek hero Herakles*, who started the Olympic Games.

* The Romans called him Hercules.

Another story claims they started as funeral games in memory of Prince Pelops of Lydia. Years before, Pelops had won a chariot race. He was racing to win a beautiful princess as his bride.

But the Games probably began as part of a big religious festival at Olympia, in praise of Zeus.

At first, there was just one event – a running race of 190m (623ft), the length of a stadium.

All the runners were Greek men. Women who wanted to race had a separate festival called the *Heraia*.

From 776BC, the Games were held at Olympia every four years, usually in August. The four-year time span between games was called an *Olympiad*.

It was the tradition in ancient Greece for male athletes to compete naked*. This gave them the chance to show off their muscular bodies.

Before their warming-up exercises, each athlete rubbed olive oil over his body. Wrestlers added powder and sand, for extra grip.

* The word 'gymnastics' comes from the Greek word *gymnos*, which means naked.

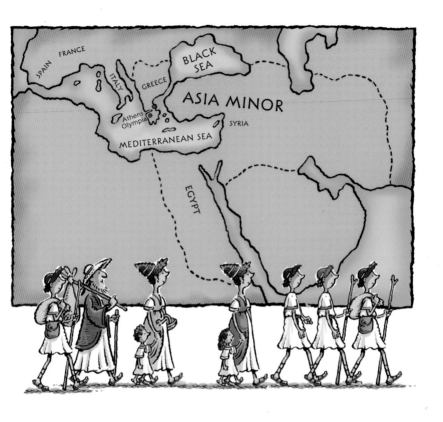

Over time, the Olympic Games became the most popular sports festival in Greece. Spectators flocked in their thousands from as far away as Italy, Syria, Egypt and the Black Sea.

13

In 456BC, a magnificent Temple of Zeus was completed at Olympia. This drew even more crowds.

People lined up to see the
fearsome 13m (43ft) high statue
of Zeus that towered inside.

Only men and unmarried women could watch the Games – on pain of death. One married woman disguised herself as a trainer to watch her son box, but she was found out when he won. Luckily, her father and brothers had all been Olympic champions, so her life was spared.

From then on, trainers had to be naked too.

Chapter 3

The show

Every fourth Spring, three heralds
journeyed around Greece to
announce a period of peace, known
as the Olympic truce, for one month
before and after the Games.

The Greeks were constantly at war but, during the truce, fighting was banned near Olympia so that people could travel to the festival in safety.

As soon as the truce was over, everyone went back to battle.

After 100 years of the Games there were 18 main events. The first was a chariot race known as the *tethrippon*, which took place in an arena called the Hippodrome.

One of the highlights was the *pentathlon*, a series of five events. According to legend, this was invented by a Greek hero named Jason, who competed in the first pentathlon against his friend, Peleus.

The pentathlon included throwing the discus...

throwing the javelin...

running...

wrestling...

and the long jump.

The most brutal event was a
savage fighting contest called the
pankration. Men could punch, kick
and break each other's bones. The
only things that weren't allowed
were biting and eye gouging.

Olympic winners were awarded a crown of olive leaves and their names were proclaimed in songs and poems throughout Greece.

When the Romans conquered Greece in the 2nd century BC, the Games were still popular.

But in AD393*, 1,166 years after the Olympics began, a Christian Roman Emperor named Theodosius I banned them. His soldiers destroyed the Temple of Zeus too.

* Dates after Christ's birth are shown by AD, which stands for Anno Domini, or 'Year of our Lord' in Latin.

Over the years, Olympia fell into ruin. After an earthquake and then a flood, the site lay buried, deep under the ground.

It remained hidden for more than 1,000 years…

Chapter 4

A grand plan

In 1875, a German archaeologist named Ernst Curtius uncovered temples, sculptures and pots among the ruins of Olympia. This sparked a wave of interest in the ancient Games.

A French nobleman, Baron Pierre de Coubertin, was fascinated by the Olympics and read everything he could about them. An enthusiastic boxer, fencer, rower and horse rider, de Coubertin believed that sports could help everyone become stronger and more successful.

He studied how sports were played in different countries. In England, he admired the fiercely competitive sports at schools such as Rugby, where rugby was invented.

He also visited a small town called Much Wenlock in England, that held a sports festival known as the *Wenlock Olympian Games.*

This sparked an idea in his mind. In 1892, at a gathering of sports officials, de Coubertin announced his plan to start an international Olympic Games.

No one listened.

De Coubertin didn't give up. He spent two more years tirelessly writing letters and talking to world leaders. Finally, he arranged another meeting of sports officials. This time, his plan was accepted. De Coubertin was thrilled.

His next job was to form a group to organize the new Olympics. This became known as the International Olympic Committee, or IOC.

Chapter 5

A successful start

The first official modern Olympic Games opened on April 6 1896, in the city of Athens in Greece.

Thousands of spectators gathered to watch male athletes from 14 countries compete in nine different sports: athletics, cycling, fencing, gymnastics, shooting, swimming, tennis, weight lifting and wrestling.

Women could only watch. In those days, many people, including de Coubertin, thought women were too delicate to play sports.

One of the biggest problems for many athletes was the journey to Athens. An American named James Connolly spent almost all his life savings on the boat trip from New York to Naples, which took 17 days.

The trip was worth it. Connolly won the hop, hop and jump (now the triple jump), and became the first medal winner in the modern Games.

The entry rules weren't very strict. An Irish tourist named John Boland signed up at the last minute... and ended up winning the tennis singles and doubles competitions.

Swimmers had to be especially tough. They had to jump out of boats into the open sea and race to shore in icy cold water.

The highlight was the marathon race of 40km (nearly 25 miles), invented for the Athens Olympics.

It was inspired by a story about a Greek soldier named Pheidippides. In 490BC, he ran this distance from Marathon to Athens, with news of Greece's victory over the Persians.

As the first marathon race at Athens drew to a close, the crowd leaped to their feet when a Greek runner named Spiridon Louis entered the stadium for the final lap.

Overcome with excitement, two Greek princes, sons of King George I of Greece, jumped onto the track and ran alongside Louis to the finish line.

Chapter 6

The Games expand

After a very successful beginning, the IOC decided to hold the Olympics every four years, in a different city each time.

In 1900, the Games were held in Paris, France. This time women could enter, but only in 'ladylike' sports, such as golf and tennis.

After the 1904 Olympics in St. Louis, USA, the IOC awarded the 1908 Games to Rome, Italy. Then Mount Vesuvius erupted and the Olympics were quickly shifted to London, UK.

For the London marathon, King Edward VII and Queen Alexandria wanted to watch the start from Windsor Castle.

So the race had to be lengthened to exactly 42.195km (26 miles 385 yards). Since then, every marathon race has been this distance.

It was at the London Olympics that people first heard de Coubertin's Olympic 'creed'— a set of ideas that summed up what he thought the Olympics were all about.

THE IMPORTANT THING ABOUT THE OLYMPIC GAMES IS NOT TO WIN BUT TO TAKE PART, JUST AS THE IMPORTANT THING IN LIFE IS NOT THE TRIUMPH BUT THE STRUGGLE...

After the 1920 Games in Antwerp, Belgium, the IOC decided there were enough sports on snow and ice to have a separate winter competition.

The first Winter Olympics took place in Chamonix, France, in 1924 and included skiing, figure skating and ice hockey. Since 1992, it has taken place two years after the Summer Olympics.

Over the years more events have been added as new sports have become more popular. In 1896 (Athens) there were 9 sports and 52 events, in 1952 (Helsinki, Finland) there were 17 sports and 149 events, and by 2004 (Athens again) there were 28 sports and 301 events.

Sports that have been added more recently include ice dancing in 1976 (Innsbruck, Austria),

beach volleyball in 1996
(Atlanta, USA),

and snowboarding in 1998
(Nagano, Japan).

BMX cycling is included in the 2008 Games in Beijing, China...

...along with a marathon 10km (6 mile) swimming race.

After the Second World War, a sports contest was held in Stoke Mandeville, England, for war veterans with spinal cord injuries.

This was a huge success and led to the first international Paralympic* Games in 1960 for athletes with disabilities.

This was followed by the first Winter Paralympics in 1976.

*_Para_ means 'alongside' in Greek.

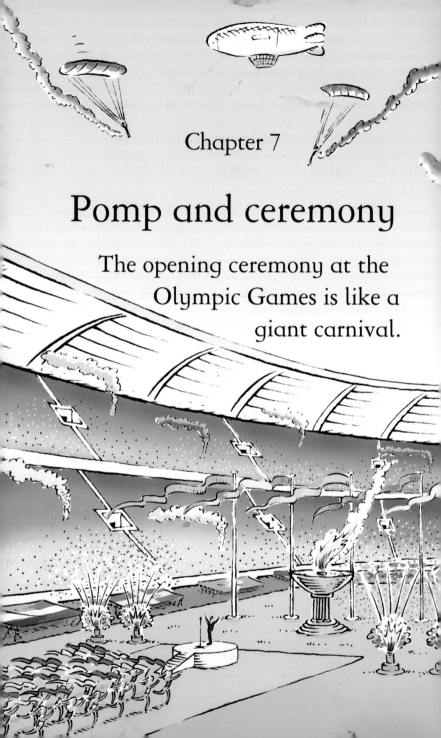

Chapter 7

Pomp and ceremony

The opening ceremony at the
Olympic Games is like a
giant carnival.

After a huge parade of athletes, there are amazing displays of music, lights, dance and fireworks.

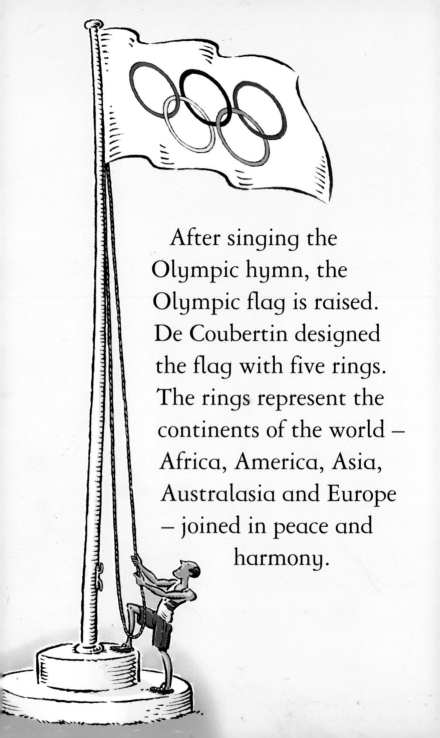

After singing the
Olympic hymn, the
Olympic flag is raised.
De Coubertin designed
the flag with five rings.
The rings represent the
continents of the world –
Africa, America, Asia,
Australasia and Europe
– joined in peace and
harmony.

Months before the Games begin, a flame is lit in Olympia and passed by a relay of torches by foot, air, road, rail or water*.

Finally, a runner brings the last torch into the stadium at the opening ceremony and lights a cauldron.

The fire burns until the end of the Games.

A flame was kept burning throughout the ancient Games, too.

* Divers have even carried a torch under the water in Australia, using chemicals that burn in water.

Chapter 8

Olympic heroes

The 1936 Olympics in Berlin took place when the Nazi leader Adolf Hitler was ruling Germany.

Hitler was eager to show off the strength of the German team, but the star of the Games turned out to be a black American runner from Ohio, called Jesse Owens.

Despite strong competition from the Germans, Owens won an outstanding four gold medals – for the 100m and 200m running races, the long jump and the 100m relay.

Owens went on to inspire many top athletes, including an American, Carl Lewis. In the 1984 Olympics, Lewis won exactly the same events as Owens.

Over four Olympic Games, Lewis won a total of nine gold medals, including an astonishing four golds in the long jump.

Lewis's nine golds matched the record of a remarkable Finnish long-distance runner Paavo Nurmi, nick-named the *Flying Finn*. Nurmi won his gold medals in the 1920, 1924 and 1928 Olympics.

A Dutch athlete, Fanny Blankers Koen, became an international hero in the 1948 London Olympics. At 30, and a mother of two, many people thought she had little chance of success. She went on to win gold in the 100m, 200m, 80m hurdles and the 4x100m relay.

One of the stars of the 1968 Olympics in Mexico City was American Bob Beamon who leaped a remarkable 8.9m (34ft) in the long jump, breaking the old world record by 55cm (22 inches).

Beamon was so shocked, he fell to his knees saying, "Tell me I'm not dreaming!"

His world record lasted 23 years.

In the 1972 Munich Olympics, the American swimmer Mark Spitz won seven gold medals and set seven world records in one week.

And at the 1976 Olympics in Montreal, Canada, 14-year-old Romanian gymnast Nadia Comaneci delighted spectators.

She was the first gymnast to score a perfect 10 points and went on to win '10' in six events. But the scoreboards weren't built for this, so her scores came up as '1's.

British rower Steve Redgrave made Olympic history at the 2000 Games in Sydney, Australia. After winning his rowing event, he became the first athlete in an endurance sport* to win gold in five Olympics.

* An endurance sport is one that is done over long distances or long periods of time.

East German canoeing star Birgit Fischer won her first gold medal at 18 in the 1980 Moscow, USSR Games. She won her eighth gold medal for Germany 24 years later, in the 2004 Athens Games – her sixth Olympics*. It was an incredible achievement.

* It could have been her seventh, but East Germany did not enter in 1984.

Today the Olympics have become the biggest sports festival in the world.

After lasting for only 100 years, who knows if the modern Games will run as long as the ancient Games, which continued for over 1,000 years.

If they do, people will still be watching and competing in the Olympics in the year 3062...

Internet links
You can find out more about the Olympics by going
to the Usborne Quicklinks Website at
www.usborne-quicklinks.com and typing
in the keyword 'Olympics'.

Please note that Usborne Publishing cannot be responsible
for the content of any website other than its own.

Dates of the
Summer Olympics

1896	Athens, Greece	1956	Stockholm, Sweden
1900	Paris, France		(horse riding events)
1904	St Louis, USA	1960	Rome, Italy
1908	London, UK	1964	Tokyo, Japan
1912	Stockholm, Sweden	1968	Mexico City, Mexico
1916	Not held (World War I)	1972	Munich, Germany
1920	Antwerp, Belgium	1976	Montreal, Canada
1924	Paris, France	1980	Moscow, USSR
1928	Amsterdam, Netherlands	1984	Los Angeles, USA
1932	Los Angeles, USA	1988	Seoul, Korea
1936	Berlin, Germany	1992	Barcelona, Spain
1940	Not held (World War II)	1996	Atlanta, USA
1944	Not held (World War II)	2000	Sydney, Australia
1948	London, UK	2004	Athens, Greece
1952	Helsinki, Finland	2008	Beijing, China
1956	Melbourne, Australia	2012	London, UK

Dates of the
Winter Olympics

1924	Chamonix, France	1972	Sapporo, Japan
1928	St. Moritz, Switzerland	1976	Innsbruck, Austria
1932	Lake Placid, USA	1980	Lake Placid, USA
1936	Garmisch Partenkirchen, Germany	1984	Sarajevo, Yugoslavia
1940	Not held (World War II)	1988	Calgary, Canada
1944	Not held (World War II)	1992	Albertville, France
1948	San Moritz, Switzerland	1994	Lillehammer, Norway
1952	Oslo, Norway	1998	Nagano, Japan
1956	Cortina d'Ampezzo, Italy	2002	Salt Lake City, USA
1960	Squaw Valley, USA	2006	Turin, Italy
1964	Innsbruck, Austria	2010	Vancouver, Canada
1968	Grenoble, France	2014	Sochi, Russia

Index

Olympics consultants:
Tony Collins and Verity Platt
Series editor: Lesley Sims
Designed by Neil Francis and Michelle Lawrence

First published in 2008 by Usborne Publishing Ltd., Usborne House,
83-85 Saffron Hill, London EC1N 8RT, England. www.usborne.com
Copyright © 2008 Usborne Publishing Ltd.